EDINBURGH BUSES AND TRAMS SINCE THE 1990S

RICHARD WALTER

Front cover: This book pays tribute to the versatile tri-axle Alexander Dennis 100 seated Euro 6 Enviro400XLB Volvo B8Ls which were delivered to Lothian Buses in 2019. Unfortunately, 1076 (SJ19 OWO), seen at Ocean Terminal new into service on 13 March 2019, sustained substantial fire damage in October 2020. Although it was beyond full repair, part of its front half was saved, repainted and donated to The Risk Factory in Edinburgh to help promote road safety awareness among schoolchildren.

Back cover: Edinburgh Trams and Lothian Buses both serve Ocean Terminal and The Royal Yacht Britannia. In this view taken on 1 April 2024, 263 is one of a number of trams vinyl wrapped to advertise the attraction. Lothian Wrightbus Gemini 3-bodied Volvo B5TL 559 (SA15 VUK) carries side adverts promoting the former floating palace.

This book is dedicated to the memory of David Mitchell (1959–2024)
Passionate about transport as an enthusiast with a long career in the Scottish bus industry and keen supporter of the Omnibus Society Scottish Branch

First published 2025

Amberley Publishing
The Hill, Stroud
Gloucestershire, GL5 4EP

www.amberley-books.com

Copyright © Richard Walter, 2025

The right of Richard Walter to be identified as the Author of this work has been asserted in accordance with the Copyrights, Designs and Patents Act 1988.

ISBN 978 1 3981 0712 0 (print)
ISBN 978 1 3981 0713 7 (ebook)

All rights reserved. No part of this book may be reprinted or reproduced or utilised in any form or by any electronic, mechanical or other means, now known or hereafter invented, including photocopying and recording, or in any information storage or retrieval system, without the permission in writing from the Publishers.

British Library Cataloguing in Publication Data.
A catalogue record for this book is available from the British Library.

Origination by Amberley Publishing.
Printed in the UK.

EU GPSR Authorised Representative
Appointed EU Representative: Easy Access System Europe Oü, 16879218
Address: Mustamäe tee 50, 10621, Tallinn, Estonia
Contact Details: gpsr.requests@easproject.com, +358 40 500 3575

Contents

Foreword by Gavin Booth		4
Introduction		6
1.	Bringing Trams Back to Edinburgh	9
2.	A Look at Edinburgh City	18
3.	East Lothian Since the 1990s	40
4.	Midlothian Developments	48
5.	The Battles to Operate in West Lothian	53
6.	Special Bus Services	60
7.	Touring Edinburgh and the Lothians	70
8.	Airport Services	80
9.	The Borders and Beyond	84
10.	The Versatile Tri-axle Deckers	87
11.	Electric Developments – Edinburgh Moves Into the Next Generation	92
Acknowledgements		96

Foreword

I realised how very different Edinburgh's bus world was in 1990 when Richard Walter asked me to provide a foreword for this book. The bus industry then was still reeling from the double whammy of deregulation in 1985 and the privatisation that followed hot on its heels. In Edinburgh the two principal operators, Lothian Region Transport (LRT) and Eastern Scottish, had co-existed for decades and both suddenly found they could flex their muscles. Eastern eyed some of LRT's city routes while LRT saw opportunities to expand beyond the city boundary into East Lothian, Midlothian and West Lothian. There followed sporadic skirmishes that became more aggressive after SMT passed into the fast-growing GRT group, soon to morph into FirstBus, where it was joined by another former Scottish Bus Group (SBG) company, Lowland, based in the Scottish Borders.

Other former SBG companies operating into Edinburgh from further afield were Fife Scottish, now part of the expanding Stagecoach empire, bringing passengers across the Forth Road Bridge, and Scottish Citylink, initially a management buyout before passing for a time to National Express.

The uncertainties of deregulation and privatisation had a knock-on effect on sales of new full-size buses. But while most operators stopped buying full-size buses and invested in minibuses, LRT bucked the trend and continued to buy full-size double-deckers; its 1991 delivery of thirty-six Leyland Olympians was one of the largest orders placed in the UK that year. This stood it in good stead to fight back when SMT and First introduced services competing with Lothian's at the same time as Lothian was expanding its network beyond the Edinburgh city boundary. Over a number of years there were bursts of tit-for-tat competition, but ultimately First pulled out of East Lothian in 2016 and West Lothian in 2022 to concentrate its resources elsewhere.

This allowed Lothian to create new brands – East Coast Buses and Lothian Country – to serve areas well beyond Edinburgh, and there was a new coaching arm, Lothian Motorcoaches, with a fleet of upmarket vehicles.

Lothian Region Transport became Lothian Buses in 2000 and responded to competition for its popular tours programme and airport service by acquiring the Edinburgh business of Guide Friday, as well as a new local operator, Mac Tours. More recently, Lothian faced competition from McGill's Bright Bus brand.

At the same time, thoughts had been turning to new tramways. Blackpool was still the only operational urban tramway in 1990, but Manchester Metrolink was under construction and would open in 1992, to be followed by five more new systems over the next twenty-five years, notably the new Edinburgh Trams, which started operating between York Place and the airport in 2014 and were extended north to Leith and Newhaven in 2023.

Scottish Citylink still operates express services alongside National Express and newcomers FlixBus and Ember. Borders Buses provides links between Edinburgh and the Scottish Borders and Houston's now operates the routes to Dumfries.

And there had been major changes in the bus-building industry. Lothian's main chassis supplier, Leyland, had been subsumed into Volvo and while new names appeared, like Optare and Wright, long-established UK-based names rose to the challenge, like Alexander and Dennis.

And, of course, buses have totally changed. The first low-floor single-deck and double-deck models appeared in the 1990s and Lothian invested in these from 1999. These were diesel-engined, and the first moves away from pure diesel were the diesel-electric hybrids bought in 2011 and more recent investment in pure electrics, which means that the buses of the mid-2020s are very different to the buses of 1990.

Richard Walter is an old friend who has travelled extensively around the UK to record the ever-changing bus scene, and this book portrays the many changes in ownership, liveries and bus design in and around Edinburgh. It reminds us how the bus business has dealt with past difficulties, some of its own making, how it has risen to the challenges and how it is grasping the opportunities of the present day.

Gavin Booth, October 2024

Moving towards a target of net-zero emissions by 2035, new MCV-bodied Volvo BZLs started to enter service during late 2024. Gleaming in the sun and being waved at by a young potential bus enthusiast on 10 September 2024 is 704e (SF74 YMA) approaching the Royal Infirmary of Edinburgh terminus of service 24.

Introduction

The Purpose of this Book

The big question is how do you capture the last thirty years or so of changes in a city as big and diverse as Edinburgh in one book with around 180 images? The answer is: you don't. I've had many tough decisions to make in the compilation of this book. I was born in Edinburgh and have lived for some years in East Lothian, so my appreciation of public transport in the region started a long time ago. I started taking photos of it in the late 1970s/early 1980s. In my previous Edinburgh work, *Lothian Buses: 100 Years and Beyond*, I concentrated on the operator Lothian Buses and its predecessors. Now, I delve a little wider into the whole Edinburgh scene, looking not just at Lothian developments but also at a sample of other service providers since deregulation. And, of course, I am including photos of Edinburgh Trams and looking at the history of the much-troubled reintroduction of a system that took somewhat longer than anticipated and also ran well over the original budgets.

Despite the background, the system has expanded and successfully compliments the bus network to move people quickly, especially when there are rugby games and other large events happening. My archive of photos over the years is huge and so what I have attempted to do for this book is to try and achieve a reasonable variety of locations and vehicle types. Some of the pictures reflect the changes between the 1980s and 1990s, so you will find some examples of older vehicles and developments in here too. Wherever possible I've tried to feature scenic backgrounds, some of which have changed considerably over the years. I have had to leave out many of the photos I found on my initial trawl, so I hope to create a follow-up book in the not-too-distant future.

Much has changed, and much continues to change at the time of writing. In recent years we have experienced the serious knock-on effects of Covid-19 and the attempts to win back passengers after a serious fall in numbers. There has also been the drive towards zero emission and cleaner ways of providing transport. Edinburgh has perhaps been slightly slower off the mark than other cities across Scotland and the UK to embrace electric or hydrogen buses, but during 2024 it saw expansion of electric services through Ember offering a choice of electric routes from Edinburgh to other Scottish cities and Lothian ordering fifty electric vehicles, its Central garage having been transformed with a number of charging facilities provided. Demand for out-of-town routes remains high, but some areas have suffered from less choice.

Looking Backwards and Forwards

There were once essentially two main providers of buses in the capital: Lothian Region Transport and Eastern Scottish. The latter was to become First, with operations split between West Lothian, East Lothian and Midlothian. In more recent years all their services migrated into either East Coast Buses or Lothian Country (part of the Lothian network) or the large

McGill's Buses group, although there were to be shake ups there in 2023. Lothian and its predecessors saw competition on its airport service from Guide Friday and more recently from McGill's Bright Bus operations, while their city open-top tours also had to contend with new tours being offered from Bright Bus and also from Guide Friday, MacTours and Rabbie's for a while. Even the city network of Lothian routes (which haven't really seen much major change in recent years) has had its 'intruders' too, most of which were short-lived like Edinburgh Transport and Lothian Transit. In the east and Midlothian regions companies like Eve's of Dunbar (taken over by Lothian in 2024) and Prentice of Haddington have run local services. In the west, firms like E. M. Horsburgh provided local services too, but demand, resources and assistance from the local council has always made this a challenging area for service provision.

Edinburgh Transport began operations in July 1990 as an offshoot of Silver Coach Lines. It ran out of the SCL depot in Salamander Street. Services operated at the start were the 133 (Edinburgh–Haddington), 330 and 331 (Dalkeith–Kinnaird Park) and 333 (South Gyle–Tranent). It also, from 1992, had the contract to operate the Forth Ferries shuttle from Granton Harbour to St Andrew Square (service 333) but this stopped when the ferry ended. Stevenson's of Uttoxeter took a controlling stake in Edinburgh Transport during 1993. By then the 133 and 330/331 had both been lost on retendering. Gained were the 15/325 (St Andrew Square–Penicuik), the southern end of what had been LRT services 15/15A. It was around then that the depot moved to Sir Harry Lauder Road. Stevenson's was taken over by British Bus in 1994, and with it they gained Edinburgh Transport, but this period was brief and by the year end it had been sold to Grampian Regional Transport. Only the services changed hands, though, and no vehicles were involved. The 315/325 subsequently passed to Lowland and what had been the 333, now the 93, passed to Lothian Transit and was withdrawn at Easter 1995.

Lothian Transit arose out of the services (10, 16 and 73) that Murray Shepherd had run in Edinburgh. Shortly before the 10 finished in August 1992, Murray bought out Stewart's of Dalkeith and relocated the business to Newtongrange, where it remained based until the end in 1996. Lothian Transit ran a Cockpen circle as service 10 and there was also a service 88 in the Portobello area. During 1993 Lowland took a stake in Lothian Transit and vehicles were then numbered in an 11xx series. Vehicles were also transferred from the main Lowland fleet, though Lothian Transit remained a separate company. It changed hands again in 1994 when Lowland was bought by Grampian Regional Transport. Its later years were as a low-cost unit – the closure of Lothian Transit and of the Newtongrange premises came at the end of March 1996 as part of the reorganisation which saw SMT split up and its fleet and depots split between Lowland and Midland Bluebird.

So, this book is a colourful salute to just some of the successful (and not so successful) attempts to keep people moving around Lothian. I do hope that you enjoy these pictorial memories and will forgive me that inevitably some events, vehicles, liveries and companies have had to be missed out. Edinburgh remains a popular destination for bus and coach enthusiasts and photographers. There is always something of interest happening and many like me venture away from the obvious locations to capture buses in more scenic and unusual locations. Please forgive the quality of some of the earlier pictures; scanning has not always done the original transparencies justice.

Richard Walter, October 2024

Former Doig's of Glasgow Caetano-UVG Urbanstar-bodied Dennis Dart SLF A01 (V664 FPO) was converted and used as a mobile ticket office and for other company publicity. In this view, taken on 30 August 2014, the bus was out and about in Haddington, East Lothian promoting Transport for Edinburgh with this eye-catching and clever vinyled livery featuring buses and trams. The bus wore two other promotional liveries for Lothian Buses during its time with the company.

In more recent years Lothian built up a large fleet of Volvo B9TL Wrightbus Eclipse Gemini 2s, such as 952 (SN11 EAA) seen on 10 November 2023 at Eastfield terminus on service 19 in one of many all-over vinyl wraps that are now a popular form of advertising.

1
Bringing Trams Back to Edinburgh

Transport for Edinburgh (TfE) is the parent company of the municipally owned Lothian Buses and Edinburgh Trams and holds the city's shares in these companies. It is responsible for the delivery and development of an integrated transport network for the Edinburgh city region. For a while both buses and trams carried the TfE identity, as seen here on Lothian Buses Wrightbus Gemini 3 Volvo B5TL 424 (BN64 CSY), seen at Gogar Tram Depot on 5 March 2017.

Trams originally operated in Edinburgh from 1871 to 1956. When the last and suitably decorated electric tram operated in the capital on 16 November 1956 few could imagine that, following a proposal from Edinburgh Council for a modern tram network in 1999, a new tramway would be officially opened on 31 May 2014. The mock-up tram seen here at Ocean Terminal was one of a number on display prior to the opening, with others in the city centre, Constitution Street, the Gyle Shopping Centre and at Edinburgh Airport.

The service is operated by Edinburgh Trams Ltd, a wholly owned subsidiary of Transport for Edinburgh. It is equipped with twenty-seven seventy-eight seated and 170 standing CAF Urbo low-floor trams numbered 251–77 that were specially designed for use in the capital. They were built in Beasai, Spain, between 2009 and 2011.

A static tram on the left is passed by one on trial in St Andrew Square, Edinburgh. The construction of the first phase, linking Edinburgh Airport with Newhaven, began in June 2008 but encountered highly publicised substantial delays and cost overruns. Indeed, a fifteen-year contract for the operation and maintenance of the network by Transdev was cancelled in 2009 and not long after there was pressure on the whole project being cancelled.

A special opportunity arose on 13 March 2014 for members of the public to apply for tickets to try out the trams between Murrayfield and Haymarket. This proved to be a very popular event, with tickets disappearing very fast.

The network officially rolled out on 31 May 2014, but initially only between Edinburgh Airport and York Place. Fares and ticketing were integrated with Lothian Buses, but services to the airport were more expensive on the trams.

Tram 256 is seen at Gogar Depot on 5 March 2017. Just seventeen trams were initially required and an unsuccessful attempt was made to lease ten to Transport for London for use on their Tramlink service.

Trams 270 and 260 at Gogar Depot, which is ideally situated on the outskirts of Edinburgh, close to Edinburgh Airport and next to the Edinburgh Gateway station, which opened in December 2016. The station provides an interchange between Edinburgh Trams and ScotRail services to Fife and Aberdeen.

255 approaching Edinburgh Park on 5 March 2017.

The tram mock up at Edinburgh Airport has been converted into a departure lounge, with seating and timetable information, seen here unusually quiet on 19 January 2024.

Vinyl advertising for all sorts of products and events has been popular on trams and brings in an attractive income to Edinburgh Trams. In this view of 251 taken on 5 March 2017 the Trainspotting advert is actually a clever promotion for Edinburgh Trams.

Edinburgh Council approved an extension of the line to Newhaven in March 2019, with construction work commencing in November of that year. This view of Ocean Terminal, taken on 4 April 2012, shows how different the landscape was before the tramline was extended and housing built opposite the shopping centre.

Jump forward to 17 August 2024 and the same view is almost totally unrecognisable, with trams and buses both serving Ocean Terminal. Construction work had commenced in November 2019 and was completed on schedule in June 2023 despite being delayed for three months by the Covid outbreak. Tram 257 can be seen carrying an advert for the 2024 Edinburgh International Book Festival.

Tram 261, seen in St Andrew Square on 3 July 2024, was given vinyls for Edinburgh Bus Tours in partnership with Edinburgh Trams, allowing passengers visiting the capital to see what tours were on offer to them.

The impressive background as Tram 271 approaches Ocean Terminal on a sunny day on 12 April 2024.

A view showing the whole length of Tram 272 as it swings into York Place on 17 May 2014. Frequent accidents involving cyclists getting their wheels stuck in the rails or skidding on them have been reported and sadly there have been collisions with pedestrians and traffic including some fatalities. There have also been power problems and trams breaking down, causing disruption. Generally speaking, though, the trams have provided a safe and reliable transport system to complement the excellent bus services in Edinburgh.

Whilst many trams only carry partial vinyl side ads, Tram 274 is one of a few to display a full vinyled advert for the Royal Yacht Britannia and is seen passing Tower Place at Leith on 1 April 2024. After this photograph was taken, this tram (and other ones with vinyl wraps) were given white stripes down the side of all doors for health and safety purposes to ensure passengers could locate the doors easily.

Tram 264, carrying an advert for The Real Mary King's Close Heritage Visitor Attraction, is seen heading towards the Newhaven terminus on 4 September 2024. As of the time of writing an additional extension serving the north–south axis of the city was in the planning stages. The troubled construction of the first phase of the network was subject to a lengthy formal enquiry which concluded that the failings by Edinburgh Council and others were largely to blame for the construction delays.

2
A Look at Edinburgh City

Acquired from Midland Scottish in December 1991, where it was fleet number 5, this former 1978 Grampian Transport Leyland National 158 ASV (previously their 58 (OLS 805T)) was withdrawn in April 1994, passing in December 1994 to Lothian Transit Ltd of Newtongrange. It transferred to Lowland Omnibuses Ltd of Galashiels in April 1996, being renumbered 18 later that year, and was withdrawn from service by September 1997. The photo shows it at Picardy Place whilst with Lothian Transit on their service 93, which ran to South Gyle as the paper notice in the front window shows.

Bright Bus is not the only orange operator that Edinburgh has seen. Back in the early 1990s, Edinburgh Transport, part of Stevenson of Uttoxeter, ran this DAF Delta ET301 (G785 PWL) on service 333 to Craig Park and Asda from South Gyle. Corgi Original Omnibus produced a 00-scale model of it as their 42907.

Eastern Scottish 1984 Leyland Olympian ONLXB/1R LL138 (A138 BSC) on City Sprinter service C16 to Oxgangs photographed at Morningside station advertising 'Lewis Upholstery'.

Alexander Dodge 50 minibus 455 (E455 JSG) on a wintry day in Oxgangs on service C1. It was one of seventy such vehicles to enter service upon deregulation of buses in October 1986 on various C-prefixed route numbers (C1–C9) carrying the City Sprinter banding trying to compete with Lothian Region Transport on the busier routes within the city limits. Some closely mirrored sections of LRT routes and at the start the C5 operated on a five-minute frequency between Clovenstone and Restalrig. LRT retaliated by extending services out of the city boundary and Eastern Scottish therefore made no significant inroads to the city market. The City Sprinter network was scaled down by the end of 1994 following a deal with LRT which saw them pull out of West Lothian.

An example of pointless bus wars hitting Edinburgh. Lothian Region Transport 1991 Leyland Lynx II 187 (H187 OSG) is seen here hotly pursued by Lothian Transit Alexander Y type Leyland Leopard HCS 817N (formerly Northern Scottish NPE3). The later had started up duplicate service 10s between St Andrew Square and Torphin and LRT retaliated with their own duplicate vehicles running wherever possible immediately before the Lothian Transit one.

Lothian Region Transport made good use of a batch of versatile 1981 Midibus Duple Dominant-bodied Leyland Cub CU435s. 169 (HSC 169X) is seen in use here on a very wintry day as a connecting service on route 16 between Oxgangs and Redford Road during roadworks where larger buses were unable to use the roads. The front-engined Cub was developed from the Terrier truck and was built at Leyland's Bathgate plant in West Lothian.

The same vehicle, LRT Midibus Duple Dominant-bodied Leyland Cub CU435 169 (HSC 169X), was subsequently repainted into a more traditional madder and red livery and given the MaxiTaxi branding. It is photographed heading to Turnhouse on service 48.

A solid product of the 1980s. Lothian Region Transport 1988 Alexander RH Leyland Olympian ONCL10RX 300 (E300 MSG) was photographed on Princes Street on service 26 when new. Leyland, and subsequently Volvo Olympians, continued to be purchased by LRT throughout the 1990s. In later years, 300 would become an open topper for the Edinburgh Classic Tour and be named *Scottish Star*.

Lothian Region Transport also bought a large number of Leyland National 2 NL116TL11/2Rs. 143 (B143 KSF) was caught on service 38 at Morningside. On the lower panels there is advertising for summer express coach services operated by LRT.

Not usually short of buses, Lothian Buses needed to acquire fourteen second-hand Leyland Nationals during 2001, including this 1979 Leyland National 1135A/1R 132 (WBN 480T) from Birmingham Omnibus Tividale. Pictured on Eskview Terrace in Musselburgh, the bus was on service 45. It was withdrawn during 2003.

Now in preservation is Lothian Buses 1982 Alexander RH-bodied Leyland Olympian ONTL11/1R 667 (GSC 667X). It was one of a pair that principally ran on services 10 and 24 in their early years. In 1987 the other vehicle, 666, was destroyed in an arson attack and was broken up for spares. This photo was taken in St Andrew Square, now a main stopping place for Edinburgh Trams rather than service buses which serve the other side of the square.

One of the earliest LRT Lothian routes to venture out of the city boundary was service 61, operated jointly with Eastern Scottish, from St Andrew Square bus station to Balerno. ECW Leyland Olympian ONTL11/2R 789 (C789 SFS) has passed the boundary in this photograph on a sunny winter's morning. LRT bought a total of 128 such dual-doored vehicles between 1982 and 1986 (668–794), with 770 allocated twice when the original was sold back to Leyland as a demonstrator.

In 1999, Lothian Region Transport took delivery of its first low-floor buses, which were also the first to feature a new harlequin livery. Pictured at the Ocean Terminal launch of the first five Alexander ALX400-bodied Dennis Tridents is 501 (T501 SSG), route branded for service 44. After a few weeks in service, the upper front panels by the destination screen were painted poppy red. Further deliveries would feature Plaxton President bodywork. All of the Alexander vehicles would later become open toppers in the City Sightseeing fleet.

Lothian Region Transport bought ninety-one Plaxton Pointer Dennis Dart SLFs between 1999 and 2003. 172 (V172 EFS) is shown on service 22 at the original Leith terminus whilst the Ocean Terminal shopping centre was under construction. The 22 was extended temporarily to the front of the Scottish Executive offices at Victoria Quay until the shopping centre opened and official terminal point was completed.

Lothian Region Transport Plaxton President Dennis Trident 576 (W576 RSG) at the old Greendykes terminus of service 21 before new housing was developed. Buses now use a bus gate to reach the Royal Infirmary of Edinburgh where they terminate.

Lothian Region Transport bought seven Plaxton President Volvo B7TLs (291–97 – the last being a former demonstrator) in 2000. 294 was snapped at Marine depot prior to entering service. It is seen with (correct) registration W294 PFS, but there was a mix up with a Travel West Midlands bus, which carried the registration W122 DOP. When the error was realised, the buses had to temporarily swap registrations until both could use their intended marks.

The Lothian harlequin livery was simplified with less (and bigger) gold and red diamonds for future orders. Wearing the revised application is Wright Eclipse Volvo B7RLE 104 (SN04 NGG), which also incorporates Night Bus branding on service 30 in Musselburgh High Street on 6 June 2009. The bus would later become driver trainer TB104 in an all-yellow livery.

Passing Chambers Street and the National Museum of Scotland is Plaxton Pointer Dennis Dart SLF 73 (SK52 OJT) on service 67 to the Bush on 12 August 2010.

Looking very smart in its harlequin livery is Lothian Buses Wright Eclipse Gemini Volvo B9TL 925 (SN08 BYV) approaching Cameron Toll on Old Dalkeith Road whilst on a service 33 on 29 July 2011. The bus carries 'Your locally owned buses', which flashes on the upper panels.

Wearing service 22 Connect branded livery at Ocean Terminal on 1 September 2009 is Lothian Buses 327 (SN09 CVH). For some considerable time service 22 (regularly receiving the most up to date buses on it) provided a frequent and well used direct link between Ocean Terminal and the Gyle Centre but when the trams started serving both locations it terminated at Waterloo Place initially and now goes to Granton Harbour via Queensferry Street.

A rather unusual and quite striking photo of James Bond's *Skyfall* offside vinyled Lothian Buses Wright Eclipse Gemini Volvo B9TL 902 (SN08 BXR), taken on 13 October 2012 with Edinburgh Castle in the background.

During 2004, prior to ordering Scania OmniCities for Airlink duties, Lothian Buses trialled East Lancs-bodied OmniDekka demonstrator SN04 CPE, numbering it 999 and decking it out in fleet harlequin livery. The bus was principally used on the busy cross-city service 37.

Leader of the Pack service 29 branded Lothian Buses Wright Eclipse Volvo B7RLE 160 (SN57 DDF) photographed at Danderhall on 25 October 2007 on service 49 to the Jewel. The 49 is another service that has seen changes to its route over the years. It now operates between the Royal Infirmary of Edinburgh and Fort Kinnaird with double-deck buses.

Freshly delivered and gleaming on service 2 in this night shot at Asda, the Jewel, on 6 February 2009, is Lothian Buses Wright Eclipse 2 Volvo B7RLE 168 (SN58 BYV).

A new livery to replace the harlequins appeared in April 2010, which was basically the traditional madder and white colours but in swoops rather than the lined style. Lothian Buses Wright Eclipse Gemini Volvo B7TL 725 (SN55 BMV), with details on its side advertising how the public could leave comments on the new livery, leaves the Greenbank terminus of service 23 on 7 April 2010.

Painted up at the same time as 725, similar Lothian Buses Wright Eclipse Gemini Volvo B7TL 720 (SN55 BLV) passes by Lady Road on 8 April 2010 but with branding for service 3 Connect. The yellow remained but branding changed for subsequent repaints to Lady Victoria Colliery at Newtongrange, as seen on page 51.

Lothian Buses Scania OmniDekka CN94UD 986 (SN57 DAO) in fleet livery photographed on service 35 at South Gyle on 27 March 2012. Visible onboard are the high-back leather seats retained from its time as an Airlink bus.

Pictured in the attractive grounds of Craig House Campus of Edinburgh Napier University on 23 July 2011 is newly delivered Lothian Buses Wright Eclipse Gemini 2 Volvo B9TL 366 (SN11 EBV). The grounds have had housing developed within them and buses ceased entering or terminating there. Service 23 now serves the former 41 terminus at Greenbank.

Coming into Straiton Retail Park on 7 October 2012 on service 37 to Penicuik is Lothian Buses Wright Eclipse Gemini 2 Volvo B9TL 811 (SN56 AGO) in The Pen-Y-Cog livery.

Looking immaculate at Marine garage on 4 April 2009 is just delivered Lothian Buses Wright Eclipse Gemini 2 Volvo B9TL 303 (SN09 CTU). Before entering service, the bus would receive Edinburgh Zoo panda vinyls rather than harlequins.

When no longer required for Skylink duties, Lothian Buses Wright Eclipse Gemini 3 Volvo B5TL 432 (SA15 VTL) retained its livery but was used on regular Lothian bus services. The photo was taken at Blackford station on 24 February 2021 when operating service 41 to Cramond.

A variety of buses were painted in simplified lined rather than swoop-style liveries including Lothian Buses Wright Eclipse Gemini Volvo B7TL 722 (SN55 BLZ) on service 25 in Princes Street on 27 June 2016.

Another different adaptation of the Lothian Buses livery on Wright Eclipse Urban Volvo B7RLE 134 (SN55 BJU), seen at Crewe Toll on service 24 on 10 August 2017. The bus in full Lothian Buses livery was modelled by Corgi on service 1 with choice of destinations – OM46015A Easter Road and OM46015B Clermiston.

After being demoted from Airlink duties, Lothian Buses Wright Eclipse Gemini 3 Volvo B5TL 498 (SF17 VOO) retained its livery but gained Skylink fleet names for use on services 200 and 400. It also appeared on normal service work from time to time. In the photo on 20 May 2020 it was working a Covid-linked duty and was leaving Asda, the Jewel, as a part route 2 to Surgeon's Hall, where it would change to a 41.

They do look good when new! Here are a few more examples of new or repainted buses. A slightly modified livery without lower panel gold lining was introduced by Lothian Buses during the Covid period. Seen in this style on 1 July 2022 is former poppy-wrapped Wright Eclipse Gemini 3 Volvo B5LH 551 (SA15 VUB) at Lochend on service 34 to Heriot Watt University.

Lothian Buses Wright Eclipse Gemini 2 Volvo B9TL 930 (SNO CVR) pulls out from Seafield works on 9 June 2009 having had all of its inspections completed and ready for service. The bus is now with Lothian Country Buses.

First day in service for Lothian Buses Alexander Dennis integral Enviro E400H diesel-electric hybrid 205 (SN61 BBF) on 10 September 2011 as it reaches the (then) terminus of service 10 at Torphin.

Heading out from Seafield Works and reaching Kings Road on 1 October 2021 ready for service is Lothian Buses ADL Enviro400 MMC Volvo B5TL 657 (SJ71 HJK).

Freshly repainted into the latest livery style having originally been with Lothian Country is Lothian Buses Wright Eclipse Gemini 2 Volvo B9TL 1028 (LXZ 5413) on service 4 to Queen Margaret University. The bus was new to Centrewest in October 2010 as BF60 VHW (VN37916) and also ran with Metroline as VW1868.

Given a new lease of life in 2023 was Lothian Buses Wright Eclipse 2 Volvo B7RLE 180 (SN13 BEY) on a revised route for service 48 into Musselburgh. It was pictured at Stoneybank on 29 May 2023. The bus had previously spent some time with Lothian Country.

All-white Lothian Buses Wright Eclipse Gemini Volvo B9TL 905 (SN08 BXV) heading for Marine on service 45 with a screen that can barely be read. The bus had previously been in orange and red for the 3 Bridges Tour.

Lothian Buses MCV eVora Volvo B8RLE 86 (SJ70 HNY) on a snowy but sunny day at Stoneybank on 9 February 2021 whilst on service 30.

Edinburgh Coach Lines is primarily a coach company, but had a contract to run bus service 13 in Edinburgh. Showing an older style of livery is Plaxton Centro 632 (SN09 FUY) heading along Queensferry Street on 30 March 2012. McGill's Buses operated the service from December 2024.

A more recent delivery in revised livery for Edinburgh Coach Lines is MCV eVora Volvo B8RLE SN19 FJA heading along Princes Street on service 13 on 18 May 2023. The bus was new to the Crowne Plaza Hotel in Dublin in April 2019 as 191-D-37522 for airport shuttle services.

3
East Lothian Since the 1990s

An unscreened (but in service) First Northern Counties Palatine II V47 Volvo Olympian 34047 (P247 UCW) with First East Scotland (formerly with London Centrewest and First West Yorkshire Halifax) on Musselburgh High Street on 27 May 2012.

First East Scotland Plaxton Pointer 2 Dennis Dart SLF 40945 (R231 SBA) leaving Musselburgh on 7 October 2010 on service 141 to Fort Kinnaird. The Dart was a common site in Musselburgh during this era, with both First and Lothian operating them on East Lothian services.

First East Scotland Transbus Plaxton President Volvo B7TL Dennis Trident 33131 (LT02 ZBX) photographed on 4 July 2013 carrying very prominent fleet names in Musselburgh High Street heading to North Berwick.

E&M Horsburgh-branded Optare Solo MH08 EMH on Pinkie Road on 18 April 2014 providing a link (T1/T2) from Musselburgh and Wallyford to Tesco Musselburgh.

Eve Coaches of Dunbar operated service 128 to the Royal Infirmary of Edinburgh at Little France via Fort Kinnaird. Shown here is Optare Solo M880 E28 (YJ11 OHW) on 9 August 2011 at Stoneybank. It was later registered to K10 EVE. The company was sold to Lothian Buses in February 2024 but has retained its identity and livery.

Originally known as East Lothian Buses.com when Lothian Buses stepped in to provide services after First East Scotland withdrew from Musselburgh and North Berwick, Plaxton President Dennis Trident 639 (SK52 OGX) was one of several buses painted all-over white. It is seen here in George Street on 20 June 2012 on service 113 between the Western General Hospital and Pencaitland but in this case working a part-route journey to Eastfield.

The unit was to become East Coast Buses on 28 July 2016 with a new livery of green and grey adopted, as shown on Plaxton President Dennis Trident 20624 (SN51 AYH) passing Wallyford Park & Ride on 3 May 2017 returning from a morning school run of service 127 to Longniddry.

Wrightbus-bodied Volvo B5LH 551 (SA15 VUB) had been painted in all-over white by 15 July 2018 when it was loaned to East Coast Buses and captured passing Asda at the Jewel on service X5 to Gullane.

Arriving at Ocean Terminal on 11 March 2012 is First East Scotland Marshall-bodied Dennis Dart SLF 41342 (T342 ALR) on a short-lived extended service 129 via Portobello, connecting the people of East Lothian with the shopping centre.

East Coast Buses operate services in Midlothian too. Wright Eclipse Urban Volvo B7RLE 10104 (RIG 6494) (new to Kent Council in March 2006 as GN06 EVM and used by Arriva Kent Thameside as their number 3808 before being acquired by East Coast Buses) reaches Midlothian Community Hospital on local Dalkeith service 139 on 10 July 2018.

East Coast Buses Wright Eclipse Gemini 2 Volvo B9TL 945 (SN10 DKX) was one of the last examples to be repainted from green and grey. It is seen here leaving Queen Margaret University on 29 May 2023 on service 106 to Haddington. For a while the service was curtailed at QMU rather than Fort Kinnaird, but since mid-2024 it now serves the Fort again, albeit via QMU.

Prentice of Haddington operate a number of eco-friendly ADL Enviro200 buses that meet low-carbon bus status as they produce 30 per cent less greenhouse gases than a standard bus. An example is 412 (YX70 OLW), pictured at Olivebank on 2 March 2021 on service 108 to Fort Kinnaird. Note the blue destination display, which was trialled but later changed to a traditional white.

Freshly repainted into the latest East Coast Buses livery, this picture shows Wright Eclipse 2 Urban Volvo B7RLE 199 (LB62 BUS) at Olivebank on service 106 on 18 May 2023.

Prior to the formation of East Coast Buses in 2016 following the withdrawal of First East Scotland from Musselburgh and North Berwick depots, the name used on services in East Lothian was Lothian Country Buses. The Lothian Country identity is now used for vehicles operating in West Lothian. Wrightbus Eclipse Urban Volvo B7RLE 174 (SN60 EOG) displays the livery and branding used when photographed near Wallyford on 13 September 2014.

A very scenic background on 19 July 2024 for East Coast Buses Wright Eclipse Gemini 2 Volvo B9TL 939 (SN10 DKJ) at Wolfstar, Ormiston, showing off the company's attractive green and white livery.

East Coast Buses bought a batch of high-spec 13.2-metre Wright Eclipse Urban 3 Volvo B8RLEs with leather seats, originally for service 124 before being displaced by higher capacity B5TIs. Now in the current green and white livery on 20 August 2024 is 58 (SF17 VMG) making its way to Fort Kinnaird via Queen Margaret University on service 106.

4
Midlothian Developments

Following the deregulation of bus services in 1986, LRT Lothian expanded its routes throughout the Lothians with service 80 venturing into Midlothian. Leyland National 2 NL116TL11/2R 149 (B149 KSF) negotiates a steep slope heading to Polton Mill. After its withdrawal from service 149 it was converted into a mobile youth project vehicle.

Lothian Transit was a short-lived operation set up in 1993 which was made up of a number of second-hand bus types, mainly Stevenson of Uttoxeter vehicles but soon replaced by Lowland vehicles. They also operated former Grampian 1967 Alexander Leyland Atlantean PDR1/1 GRS 118E. The company ceased trading in late 1994 as Lowland wanted the maintenance facilities at Gala depot and First bought Lothian Transit out.

Approaching Tesco, Hardengreen near Dalkeith, on 4 June 2012 is Lothian Buses Wrightbus Eclipse Urban Volvo B7RLE 157 (SN57 DCZ) with the second of two special branded liveries for service 49, which became *The Queen of Scots*.

Munro's of Jedburgh was a bus company that operated local and regional bus services in the city of Edinburgh, East Lothian, Midlothian and the Scottish Borders. It was closed in July 2013 following a retendering exercise by Scottish Borders Council. One of its MAN eVolutions, AE06 VPU, is seen entering Dalkeith on 9 June 2012 on service 52 from Jedburgh to Edinburgh.

First Scotland East Mercedes Benz Citaro 64003 (LT02 NTY) at Dalkeith on service 328 on 9 June 2012. The bus was new to First Riverside with fleet number ES64003.

For a short period in 2012, First Scotland East borrowed some vehicles from Lothian Buses to operate local routes in the Dalkeith area. Optare Solo SR 35 (SN08 BYW) was caught on service 92A on 9 June 2012 outside the now closed First depot in Dalkeith. The bus was subsequently disposed of to Bay Travel.

Wrightbus Gemini-bodied Volvo B9TL 714 (SN55 BKX) on service 3 in Dalkeith on 9 June 2012 with special branding for the Lady Victoria Colliery at Newtongrange. The venue is the home of the National Mining Museum of Scotland.

Lothian Buses Plaxton Pointer Dennis Dart SPD 176 (Y176 CFS) was another vehicle on loan to First Scotland East when the photo of it on service 92A in Dalkeith was taken on 5 June 2012.

East Coast Buses Wright Eclipse 2 Urban Volvo B7RLE 10199 (LB62 BUS) approaching Tesco, Hardengreen near Dakeith, on 25 February 2021 on local service 139. The bus was subsequently renumbered to its original fleet number of 199 and is in the green and white current livery (see page 46).

During 2018, Thorntons Bus Refurbishment of Ashington upgraded 10 of Lothian's Wrightbus Gemini-bodied Volvo B9Tls to very high coach standards for Lothian Motorcoaches duties. Subsequently they were used by Lothian Country and then East Coast Buses where they received green and white repaints. On 25 February 2021, 844 (MXZ 1754) was still in grey livery on service 140 from Musselburgh to Penicuik.

5

The Battles to Operate in West Lothian

The provision of bus services in West Lothian has been an ongoing issue for a long time. When deregulation brought SMT (the predecessor of First Scotland East) into competition within Edinburgh in 1986, Lothian responded by introducing services extending beyond the city's boundaries, including some into West Lothian. Following local government reorganisation in 1996 and First's predecessor GRT Bus Group acquiring SMT, Lothian pulled out of West Lothian and South Queensferry. Moving on into the 2000s, First Scotland East Wright Solar Scania L94UB 65752 (SN55 JVD) is seen heading from Queensferry Street onto Charlotte Square on 31 March 2012 on service 38.

First Scotland East ADL Enviro400 MMC 33431 (SN66 WGA) on Princes Street on 27 July 2018 in a blue First West Lothian livery for service 28. The bus transferred to First Glasgow in 2019 where it carried branding for service 41.

Lothian Country Plaxton Leopard Interurban-bodied Volvo B8R 9208 (SB19 GKO) complete with wheelchair lifts in Linlithgow on 15 June 2019 to promote the new express Green Arrow service into Edinburgh. The vehicle is now with Lothian Motorcoaches. In the summer of 2018, a five-phase expansion had established a Lothian Country network that linked Edinburgh with many of the main towns in West Lothian, as well as some local routes between them. The network was to be trimmed in subsequent years.

Livingston operator E&M Horsburgh Plaxton Pointer 2 Dennis Dart MPD SN06 BSO at Old Dalkeith Road on the X40 hospital connection from the Royal Infirmary of Edinburgh to St John's Hospital at Howden on 17 May 2023. Later in 2023 the service was taken over by Lothian Country with some route alterations.

All-white Lothian Country Wright Gemini 3 Volvo B5TL 571 (SJ67 MFE) leaves the Gyle Centre bound for West Lothian on 21 August 2018 on service 275. It was new to Lothian Buses in blue and white Skylink livery and was later to be painted in full Lothian Country livery.

Exiting the Gyle Centre on 21 August 2018 is Lothian Country Wright Eclipse Gemini 2 Volvo B9TL1030 (LXZ 5415) on a service 275. The bus was new to Centrewest in London in October 2010 as VN37921 (BF60 NHY) and was refurbished and converted to single door when sold to Lothian Country.

In September 2022, it was announced that McGill's Group had bought the First Scotland East business and all of its routes in the area. This included all First depots in Livingston, Larbert, Bannockburn and Balfron. Soon after vehicles from First Scotland East started to appear in new liveries, including, renumbered from 33449, ADL Enviro400 MMC 8951 (SN66 WHB). Newly painted by 26 September 2022, the bus is seen leaving Regent Road on service X24. The livery, promoted as being a retro-style Eastern Scottish livery, was actually noted as being very similar to the current Lothian Country livery and did not last long before a completely new identity was designed and introduced.

McGill's Buses Midland Bluebird Wright Eclipse Urban Volvo B7RLE 2239 (SF11 CWV) on an X38 in Princes Street on 5 July 2023 shows off the effect of the livery with added Midland Bluebird logos based on original artwork.

McGill's Buses Wright StreetLite DF 0468 (SN65 OJV) is an example of the revised Eastern Scottish livery on an X22 into Edinburgh on 5 July 2023. Neither the livery nor the route were to last for long though as in November 2023 it was announced that McGill's was to cease its bus services in West Lothian, despite an injection of some £4.5 million into Eastern Scottish to turn round the ailing business.

A similar blue and cream livery as shown on McGill's Buses Midland Bluebird Wright StreetLite DF 0448 (SN64 CJZ) photographed at Regent Road on 13 April 2023 on service X38.

Also in the latest livery is McGill's Buses Midland Bluebird ADL Enviro200 MMC 4108 (YX19 OSW) on service X38 on 27 April 2023.

Showing off the intended Eastern Scottish livery for double decks is ADL Enviro400 8974 (YX62 BGE) at Livingston Centre on a 26 on 10 October 2023. On withdrawal of the Eastern Scottish services the bus transferred to McGill's Buses Xplore Dundee fleet where it retained the livery but picked up new vinyls. The bus was new to RATP London United with fleet number ADE52.

McGill's Buses Midland Bluebird 4211 (YX19 OTN) on 27 April 2024 retains its McGill's livery but with Midland Bluebird fleet names and branding applied for service X38, as seen in this Princes Street view.

As a result of the sudden withdrawal of West Lothian Services by McGill's Buses, Lothian Country introduced some new services to fill gaps in provision and acquired some extra buses from Lothian Buses. Painted from madder and white to green and white on 3 July 2024, Wright Eclipse Gemini 2 Volvo B9TL 1050 (LXZ 5438) is leaving Regent Road on service X18 to Bathgate. The vehicle was new as dual-door First Centrewest VN37898 (BF60 UUK).

6
Special Bus Services

During July 2007 Stagecoach ran a trial hovercraft service across the Firth of Forth for two weeks between Seafield, Edinburgh and Kirkcaldy. While the amount of people eager to try out the service far outstripped expectations, the plan was sunk by Edinburgh Council. Lothian Buses provided Stagecoach with two specially decorated Volvo Olympians including 974 (L974 MSC) for the Forthfast shuttle bus service X91 between Marine bus garage and Ocean Terminal. The bus is seen on a miserable wet morning at Ocean Terminal on 16 July 2007.

Stagecoach Van Hool-bodied Astromega TD297 50144 (TSV 780), named *Sunshine* after one of the pandas that were an attraction at Edinburgh Zoo for a number of years, was one of two vehicles that operated a service between Ayr and Edinburgh stopping at Edinburgh Zoo. Between journeys the buses rested at Lothian Buses' Central Garage at Annandale Street, where the vehicle is seen departing from on 28 February 2012.

Another shuttle bus service was required when the Forth Ferries from Granton to Burntisland launched in April 1991. SMT had two Volvo Ailsa B55-10s painted up that operated between St Andrew Square and Granton Harbour. VV37A and VV38A (TSJ 597/598S) were pictured together in St Andrew Square bus station.

Eight high-spec Plaxton Leopard Interurban-bodied Volvo B8Rs were purchased for Lothian Country in 2019 for Green Arrow express services to Bathgate and Linlithgow. The services were subsequently discontinued and vehicles transferred to Lothian Motorcoaches, where they were repainted into LMC grey livery. 9205 (SB19 GKK) still in its original livery, was performing Musselburgh Races shuttles at Wallyford Park & Ride when this shot was taken on 20 August 2021.

Various bus companies have undertaken Musselburgh Races shuttles over the years picking up and dropping from Wallyford and Newcraighall station to the famous racecourse. First Scotland East used buses such as Wright Eclipse Gemini Volvo B9TL 372272 (SN57 JBV), pictured as it left Musselburgh depot on 11 June 2016. Just to confuse it was wearing a blue version of First West Lothian livery.

Alexander Dennis integral Enviro E400H diesel-electric hybrid 205 (SN61 BBF) makes the sharp turn out of Market Street onto the Mound on a short-lived service 9 between the Royal Botanic Garden and the National Museum of Scotland in Chamber Street on 7 June 2014.

In harlequin livery, but wearing MacTours fleet names, is Optare Solo M960 37 (SN08 BYZ), which was handy during roadworks at Oxgangs/Frogston when a shuttle bus was required to take passengers to Hillend on 9 August 2009. The bus would later be repainted into a version of madder and white and renumbered 280.

Similar Optare Solo M960 40 (SN08 BZC) seen on 30 March 2009 in Queen Street in one of three liveries it wore for the Standard Life Group contracted route 61. The service was intended for employees to travel between the two main headquarters at Canonmills and the West End. The bus would later be renumbered as 281.

LRT Lothian 1996 Volvo Royale-bodied Olympian 433 (P433 KSX) was given a special livery in 2000 for use on service X50 serving the original berth of the Royal Yacht Britannia at Ocean Terminal. The route was replaced by the MacTours Britannia tour and later the Majestic Tour. 433 remained in this livery, appearing on normal services – such as the 35, as pictured here – until 2004 when it was repainted into madder and white. The bus in this guise was modelled by Northcord (CMNL) as their UKBUS 4007.

LRT Lothian 1996 Volvo Royale-bodied Olympian 433 (P433 KSX) in another livery it carried for service X50 awaits passengers at Ocean Terminal in 2000.

Lothian Buses Plaxton President Dennis Trident 2 544 (V544 ESC) on Old Dalkeith Road approaching Cameron Toll on 9 July 2009 in the special service X48 livery between Ingliston and Sherifhall, which was also worn by a batch of Plaxton Dennis Darts.

A novel half and half harlequin and madder and white livery was applied to Lothian Buses Wright Eclipse Gemini Volvo B9TL 918 (SN08 BYL), seen at Shandwick Place on service 33 on 16 May 2014. The work was carried out internally by company apprentices and even the interior seat covering was split in half representing two eras of buses in the capital.

Lothian Buses have had a few themed Edinburgh Zoo buses over the years over different deliveries. Each creature is usually applied to two buses. In this photo taken on 29 July 2009, Wright Eclipse Gemini 2 Volvo B9TL 321 (SN09 CVB) was wrapped in dramatic tiger vinyls. Although primarily used on service 26 that passes the zoo, the buses strayed onto other routes as here approaching Queen Margaret University on service 45.

The arrival of two giant pandas at Edinburgh Zoo prompted this contravision advertising on Lothian Buses 2008 Wrightbus Gemini-bodied Volvo B9TL 900 (SN08 BXO). The bus is seen near Prestonpans on 12 May 2012.

As various animals and birds come and go, branding changes on the Lothian Buses' zoo bus fleet. The arrival of Cleo the cheetah in August 2024 meant that what were two sun bears-vinyled buses became cheetah buses. Wright Eclipse Gemini 3 Volvo B5TL 475 (SF17 VNL) at the terminus of service 4 at Queen Margaret University on 20 August 2024.

Lothian Buses Wrightbus Gemini-bodied Volvo B9TL 901 (SN08 BXP) was originally painted pale blue to promote awareness of male cancer, as seen here turning off Lothian Road onto the Western Approach Road on a diverted service 33 to Baberton on 6 October 2012. It subsequently advertised other things such as the company's social media channels before being repainted back into fleet colours.

Wright Eclipse Gemini 2 Volvo B9Tl Lothian Buses 350 (SN59 BHF) was one of two service 22-branded vehicles receiving additional vinyls for Edinburgh's entry in the Clipper 11-12 Round the World Yacht Race. It was captured at South Gyle on 30 July 2012.

Pictured on 30 October 2021 at Mayfield Dalkeith is Lothian Buses Wright Eclipse Gemini 3 Volvo B5LH 552 (SA15 VUC) in the special 'Scotland, Let's Do Net Zero' livery it wore during the UN Climate Change Conference in Glasgow (COP26). An Edinburgh tram wore the same vinyls.

In keeping with other operators throughout the UK, Lothian Buses have carried special liveries for Remembrance Day. Wrightbus-bodied Volvo B5LH 551 (SA15 VUB) has carried a few different versions including this one when photographed on Pinkie Road in Musselburgh on 26 April 2020 on service 26 to Tranent.

Megarear adverts together with standard side ads can be useful for various promotions. Lothian Buses 1020 (LXZ 5409) is a refurbished former London Wright-bodied Volvo B9TL and was one of four buses with slightly different advertising for the Lothian Buses and Edinburgh Trams app. The photo shows it leaving Asda at the Jewel on service 4 on 12 July 2024.

7

Touring Edinburgh and the Lothians

Edinburgh has a history of bus tours going back over the years to the early days of coaches. The open-top tours we recognise today started in 1989 with the Edinburgh Classic Tour being offered on Leyland Atlanteans 900 and 583, which were converted to fully open-top vehicles. Other Atlanteans followed (some full and some partially open top) and indeed some operated in conjunction with local operators in Cambridge and Oxford whilst later a few appeared in York. Alexander-bodied Leyland Atlantean AN68C/1R 660 (GSC 660X), new in 1981, was usually allocated to airport duties but is seen here on The Sea, the City and the Hills tour at Portobello.

MacTours was the first company to challenge the Edinburgh tour monopoly with their own city tours using a mix of vintage vehicles, later to be replaced by former London Routemasters. The company eventually merged with Edinburgh Bus Tours under the ownership of Lothian Buses in April 2002. Lothian kept the livery and fleet name but consolidated the variety of vintage types to mainly Routemasters such as 5 (JSJ 747) at Holyrood Gait on 24 April 2009. Bus services were initially retained leading to a few Lothian buses transferring and operated in MacTours livery.

The MacTours company was originally set up in 1999 by Donald and Ruth Dewar, who operated a fascinating selection of both vintage bus tours in the city and a few normal service routes. Vehicles appeared in variations of red and cream liveries and included 1958 Park Royal-bodied Leyland PD2/40 LST 873 with open rear staircase seen on Waverley Bridge. The bus was originally CEO 952 and had carried registration TRN 662A before its spell with MacTours.

Guide Friday tried their hand at Edinburgh Tours too during the mid-2000s. An example of the vehicles used was 1985 Optare-bodied Leyland Olympian C147 KBT (new to West Yorkshire PTE as their 5147), which shared the tours departure point on Waverley Bridge. Guide Friday operated The Britannia Tour as well as a City Tour and is the first in a series of photos of other buses showing how the identity of the Britannia tour has changed over the last few years. Interestingly the bus with new owners returned to Edinburgh briefly during 2023 when it provided an unusual Edinburgh Fringe venue for comedian Holly Lovelady's 'Topless' show. The vinyls for the show covered its Keighley Borough Transport tribute livery it now wears.

The first of several liveries worn on Edinburgh Bus Tours vehicles for what was called The Majestic Tour. Alexander-bodied Leyland Olympian 357 (F357 WSC) in partial open-top condition on Waverley Bridge on 3 August 2010.

Converted to open top, Plaxton President Dennis Trident 2 523 (V523 ESC) on 27 July 2011 in the next variation of the Majestic Tour livery at Ocean Terminal, which is home to the Royal Yacht Brittania and a very popular tourist destination.

This photo of Wright Gemini 3-bodied Volvo B5TL 245 (SJ16 ZZK), delivered new as an open-top bus in the last livery for the Majestic Tour, shows it at Ocean Terminal on 8 May 2023 shortly before the demolition of one of the car parks, turning to cross the tram lines.

The Majestic Tour was rebranded as the Majestic Tour during 2024. Wright Gemini 3-bodied Volvo B5TL 247 (SJ16 ZZO) turns at the roundabout by Holyrood on 31 March 2024 on the replacement Regal Tour, which follows a slightly altered route following customer feedback.

A Lothian Buses vehicle transferred into the MacTours identity in 2002 complete with cream wheels was 1984 ECW Leyland Olympian 753 (B753 GSC), photographed near Stoneybank, Musselburgh, on a rail replacement service.

During 2017, East Coast Buses borrowed some of the Edinburgh Bus Tours madder and white open-top Plaxton-bodied Dennis Tridents and used them as weekend duplicates on their busy 124 service to North Berwick. The success of this venture prompted East Coast Buses to start up a new hop-on, hop-off East Coast tour for the summer of 2018, with two open-top vehicles converted from former Scania OmniCities. Should either of the buses be off the road for any reason, the Tridents were drafted in as in the case on 6 July 2018 when 218 (XIL 1485) was assisting.

An example of the two East Coast Tour Scania OmniCities was 20944 (SN57 DCE), pictured on 6 July 2018 at Seton Sands on its early morning journey to commence duties in North Berwick. Passengers could join the tour in the morning in Edinburgh and choose to return later that day or use their ticket on any East Coast Buses service back into the city.

Showing off tartan additions to its red City Sightseeing Edinburgh livery for the 2024 season is Wright Gemini 3-bodied Volvo B5TL 231 (SJ16 CTO) on 13 March 2024 arriving at Dynamic Earth, Edinburgh's world-class Science Centre and Planetarium.

The third Edinburgh Bus Tour is the only one to offer a live commentary. The others have recorded commentaries via earphones. Wright Gemini 3-bodied Volvo B5TL 242 (SJ16 ZZF) had a makeover in 2024 to a new livery in the same style as The Regal Tour and was captured in Holyrood Park under the dramatic background of Arthur's Seat on 26 March 2024.

The first open-top conversion in the LRT Lothian fleet was Edinburgh's only long wheelbase Alexander-bodied Leyland Atlantean PDR/2/1, 900 (JSC 900E), last of a batch delivered to Edinburgh Corporation Transport (ECT) in 1967 (it was also the longest lasting Edinburgh Atlantean). It is seen in the second black and white livery it wore. Originally it had been painted mainly white with relief madder. The bus has now been preserved in traditional ECT madder and white livery and is regularly carrying passengers around the Lathalmond site of the Scottish Vintage Bus Museum.

Lothian Buses took over the Guide Friday city tour operations during 2009. Some of the Lothian open-top fleet, together with some Guide Friday ones, were painted in a new version of green and cream with Guide Friday fleet names such as Leyland Olympian 241 (previously 301) (E301MSG), seen close to Bristo Square on 25 August 2009.

Plaxton President-bodied Dennis Trident 513 (V513 VSC) in the distinctive livery of the short-lived Edinburgh World Heritage Official Tour. The commentary on the tour gave passengers a more detailed history of the 'City of Contrasts' than the other tours on offer, although most of the same tourist attractions were included.

A new venture was trialled in 2016 by Rabbie's Trail Blazers. The very first registered service (under the banner of 'rabbie's city tours') was operated using EVM Cabrio open-topped mini-coaches (with novel sliding roofs for bad weather) such as SN16 BWO on 2 June 2016. The intention was to provide a tour using small vehicles that could access interesting parts of the city that existing larger vehicles couldn't reach.

When McGill's Buses acquired the business of First East Scotland buses in 2022 they also acquired the Edinburgh open-top bus operation – Bright Bus Tours. During 2023 many of the existing open-top buses were replaced. 2908 (CKZ 35 – previously BF60 UUJ) is a Wright Eclipse Gemini 2 Volvo B9TL. The photo was taken on 8 May 2024 at the Dynamic Earth attraction.

LRT Lothian 1996 Volvo Royale-bodied Olympian 433 (P433 KSX) in yet another guise, this time for the Forth Bridges Cruise Bus and Boat Tour, leaving its Marine Garage on 1 July 2011.

Edinburgh Bus Tours Plaxton President-bodied Dennis Trident 651 (XIL 1484) was one of the next buses to be used on the Forth Bridges Cruise Bus and Boat Tour in a revised livery and was pictured on the Mound on 4 June 2016.

Rebranded as the 3 Bridges Tour is Plaxton President-bodied Dennis Trident 650 (XIL 1483) on Princes Street on 28 July 2018. 651 was in similar livery. Both were replaced by Wright Eclipse Geminis before Edinburgh Bus Tours decided to cancel the service after the 2023 summer season.

A new for 2024 Boat and Bridges Tour was started by McGill's Buses Bright Bus Tours in partnership with Forth Boat Tours. The bus used was former First West Lothian 33449 ADL Enviro400 MMC 8951 (SN66 WHB) fresh from its retro Eastern Scottish livery (see page 56). The photo was taken in St Andrew's Square on 1 June 2024 – the first day of operation.

8
Airport Services

New to Lothian Region Transport in 1982 were five single-door Alexander-bodied Leyland Atlantean AN68/1Rs in black and white livery for airport duties, which were all given the names of famous Scottish authors. 660 (GSC 660X) was *Sir Arthur Conan Doyle* until it was later repainted madder and white for regular bus service during the 1990s.

Probably my favourite airport livery was this version given to the initially branded Airline service 100. Just after repaint in 1995 from black and white livery is 1989 Alexander Leyland Olympian ONCL10/2RZ 370 (F370 WSC) loading up at Edinburgh Airport. The bus was downgraded to madder and white bus duties in 2000 and painted a lighter red and white for service 15 in 2005.

Leyland Olympians were replaced on to what were rebranded as Airlink duties by 2000 with Plaxton President-bodied Dennis Trident 2s such as 539 (V539 ESC), seen leaving the old Shrubhill works when brand new to take up service.

In the summer of 2006, 15 Scania OmniCity buses arrived for Airlink duties. 989 (SN57 DBU) enters George Street on 1 May 2009. The batch ended their service life with Lothian in madder and white on route 35 apart from two which were converted to open top and painted green and grey for East Coast Buses for a new East Coast tour for the summer of 2018 (see page 75).

Wrightbus Gemini-2-bodied Volvo B9TL 937 (SN10 DKE) heads along George Street on 5 October 2011 in another Airlink livery and style. The bus subsequently passed to East Coast Buses.

Probably the shortest-lived buses on the 100 were the 2015 batch of Wrightbus Gemini 3-bodied Volvo B5TLs 426–37, which were replaced in 2017 by similar 498–510 in a different livery (see page 33). All are now in madder and white, although 431–437 appeared in Skylink blue and white for a while. 432 (SA15 VTL) was photographed on the Mound on 4 June 2016.

At the time of writing, Airlink is operated by a batch of 100-seater Volvo B8Ls with ADL Enviro400XLB tri-axle dual-door bodywork in dark blue livery (see page 91). 1126–1130 were downgraded to bus duties during Covid and painted all-over white. During 2023, 1126 and 1127 became madder and red, whilst in 2024 1128–1130 received all-over promotional wraps for the Airlink service. 1128 (SB19 GLY) at the West End of Princes Street shows off the vinyls shortly after being treated.

A short-lived competitor for the Edinburgh Airport service in the early 2000s was tour operator Guide Friday, who ran the Airport Express. Amongst other vehicles, one of the buses used was this former London Leyland Titan, TN15 (KYV 396X), pictured on Princes Street in a dark green and cream but not standard Guide Friday livery that other vehicle types wore.

Registered as Edinburgh Shuttle Ltd, but formerly part of Lothian Buses, was this Ford Transit Minibus/Ford M7 S9 (SH56 RPX) seen on Waverley Bridge on 13 March 2009. You could pre-book a vehicle from Edinburgh into central locations, making it a taxi-style service. The vehicles ran on set routes but dropped off passengers at other destinations within a certain radius on request.

McGill's Buses Bright Bus 8486 (SN62 AOZ) is an ADL/Transbus Enviro300 new to First Glasgow as their 67751 and latterly with Midland Bluebird. The Edinburgh Airport Express service commenced on 1 January 2024 with buses running up to every fifteen minutes. 8486 was pictured on 3 January 2024 arriving at Edinburgh Airport passing a GRP 1:1 replica Spitfire which was installed in its current location when RAF Turnhouse was closed.

9

The Borders and Beyond

Borders Buses (part of the West Coast Motors Craig of Campbeltown fleet) operate a network of bus routes across the Scottish Borders, Carlisle, East Lothian, Midlothian and the Edinburgh area. Scania N230UD 11108 (YT11 LSE) passes through York Place on service X62 to Peebles having left Edinburgh bus station on 5 August 2017. It was new as a Scania demonstrator in June 2011 and appears in an early version of the fleet livery here.

Borders Buses has a fleet containing many bike-friendly buses. Customers with bikes can check the company app to track where the buses are so they can plan their journeys in advance. One of these fitted buses is ADL E40D Enviro400 MMC 11901 (SK19 ELV), pictured crossing Captain's Road in Edinburgh on 16 September 2021 on the busy X62 service to Peebles.

An unusual small bus in the Borders Buses fleet (but still carrying West Coast Motors fleet names) is AOS Grand Toro 12305 (GX23 BZK) shown at Meadowbank stadium on 29 April 2024 heading to St Boswells on service 51.

Houston's Coaches based in Lockerbie operate a number of bus services including the 101, 101A and 102 between Dumfries and Edinburgh. Pictured in Fairmilehead on 18 May 2023 is MCV eVolution-bodied Volvo B7RLE KP12 BUS formally belonging to Pulhams Coaches and still wearing that company's livery.

During 2023 Houston's Coaches upgraded its fleet in late 2023 with four MCV eVora Volvo B8RLEs. All carry names, such as *Bus Lightyear* on SJ73 HSX pictured on 13 October 2023 in St Andrew Square.

Ember fully electric tri-axle Yutong CTe12 SG24 UJC arrives in St Andrew Square on 20 June 2024 where the service from Dundee terminates. The company has an all-electric fleet of Yutong coaches operating frequent services between Dundee, Glasgow, Edinburgh, Stirling, Kinross, Edinburgh Airport and more. New connections with Aberdeen were due to commence at the end of 2024.

First Scotland East Wright Eclipse Gemini Volvo B9TL 37133 (SN57 HDH) on the X62 to Peebles at Regent Road on 11 June 2014 before the service moved to Borders Buses. Passengers could hardly miss this bus in its tartan 'Connect to the real Scotland' livery.

McGill's Buses operate many long-distance services on behalf of FlixBus but also provide a half-hourly 090 service between Glasgow and Edinburgh. Yutong GT14 coach 0565 (SG24 UHW) arrives at Regent Road during the 2024 Edinburgh Festival.

10
The Versatile Tri-axle Deckers

Probably one of the best buys for Lothian Buses in recent years has been the 100-seater Volvo B8Ls with ADL Enviro400XLB tri-axle dual-door bodywork – the first buses in Edinburgh fitted with dual doors for some twenty years. In this view from 11 December 2018, 1071 (showing its original registration number of SG68 LCN – it was registered to SJ19 OWF before entering service) is seen exiting the Royal Mile at Deacon Brodie's following a launch at Edinburgh Castle.

Before entering service, drivers were given familiarisation opportunities. 1065 (SJ19 OVY) was pictured heading into Edinburgh after a trip out to Seton Sands on type training on 8 March 2019.

Marine garage on 24 March 2019. New XLBs including 1092 (SJ19 OXH) and 1097 (SJ19 OXP) await delivery to Central as older vehicles for withdrawal transfer between garages.

Passing the Loch Fyyne restaurant at Newhaven harbour is 1095 (SJ19 OXM) on 25 March 2019. Because the buses entered service close to the company's centenary celebrations, permission was granted from Edinburgh Council to recreate the original Edinburgh Corporation Transport crests on vehicle sides. The batch also carry LothianCity fleet names. On repaint during 2024 the crests were lost but the unique fleet names remain.

Lothian provided some of its XLB to assist First Glasgow during the delayed UEFO Euro 2020 football tournament in June/July 2021 for shuttles in Glasgow to the venues there including 1112 (SJ19 OYP), duly screened up on 18 June 2021.

On service 5 nearing Brunstane on 14 April 2020 is 1069 (SJ19 OWC). As in other parts of the country, a limited bus service was provided during Covid lockdowns and Lothian operated mainly from Central garage, with its XLBs appearing on many routes they would not normally serve.

On 2 May 2020, 1079 (SJ19 OWU) appeared on a short working of the service 400 during Covid. It is seen approaching Kaimes crossroads heading to the Gyle Centre rather than Edinburgh Airport.

One of a number of XLBs used on shuttle bus duties in East Lothian for the 2024 Scottish Golf Open championships was 1083 (SJ19 OWY) approaching Longniddry Railway Station from the venue at The Renaissance Club in East Lothian on 13 July 2024.

During 2019, just prior to Covid, Lothian celebrated 100 years by outshopping 1125 (SJ19 OZD) in a special commemorative livery recognising the rich history of the company and its predecessors in Edinburgh. During the Covid lockdowns it appeared on a number of services other than its usual haunts. In this case it was pictured at the Jewel terminus of service 5 at Asda on 8 June 2020.

29 May 2020 and 1125 (SJ19 OZD) is seen leaving Restalrig on the east side of the city on a service 25 to Riccarton on the west side.

Heading through Gilmerton from Dalkeith on 15 June 2020 is 1125 (SJ15 OZD) on service 3 to Clovenstone.

After its stint in Centenary livery, 1125 (SJ15 OZD) was given a special giraffe-themed all-over wrap for Edinburgh Zoo and was pictured on service 31 near the Murrays on 15 July 2021 en route for Bonnyrigg in Midlothian.

During the Covid period, Airlink 1134 (SB19 GMV) was transferred temporarily to Lothian Motorcoaches and put into use by the NHS and Scottish Ambulance Service as a mobile vaccination centre appearing at various locations throughout the Lothians. In this view it is leaving Asda at the Jewel on 4 August 2021.

Another photo of 1134 (SB19 GMV) setting up a vaccination drop-in clinic at Fort Kinnaird in Edinburgh on 18 August 2021. All the shots in this chapter demonstrate how useful the 100-seater vehicles have been throughout their relatively short time with Lothian.

11
Electric Developments – Edinburgh Moves Into the Next Generation

In 2011, the Scottish Green Bus Funding allowed Lothian to order fifteen Alexander Dennis integral Enviro E400H diesel-electric hybrid buses. One example was 212 (SN61 BBZ) in its initial special winter gold and radiance red livery leaving its terminus at Platinum Point at Leith on 18 June 2016. The buses received a mini-refurbishment during that year inside and out into the traditional madder and white livery. All fifteen were subsequently converted to traditional diesel before the batch was eventually sold off to Wellglade Group in the English Midlands in 2022/23.

Secured through further Scottish Green Bus Funding, Lothian took delivery of fifty Volvo 7900H hybrid buses in 2013. 43 (BT64 LHY) was photographed on 18 June 2016 coming out of Musselburgh on service 45 to Riccarton, which is a route that has changed a few times in recent years. Like the decker Hybrids, the batch initially wore the gold/red livery variation but were subsequently repainted into fleet livery.

Lothian's first fully electric vehicles arrived in September 2017 in the form of a small batch of six Wright StreetAirs represented here by 288 (SK67 FLG) on service 1 at Regent Road on 11 November 2017. Based at Central garage where chargers were installed, the buses didn't stay in service for long, but at the time of writing are still in storage and have not been sold on.

Thanks to major funding from SP Energy Networks Lothian introduced four all-electric ADL Enviro400EV buses in June 2021. The £1.7 million project was funded as a flagship project of SP Energy Networks' £20 million Green Economy Fund to enable Edinburgh to take a major step in its journey towards the city becoming net zero by 2030. 292 (LG21 JDJ) in the vehicles' distinctive green livery was pictured near the Bonaly terminus of service 10 on 27 June 2021.

In 2024, following trials with a demonstrator from Volvo, Lothian Buses launched the first of fifty MCV Volvo BZL Electric buses, initially operating on the service 8 and 9 routes. The buses offer customers improved comfort and quieter journeys, with each accommodating more than seventy passengers and featuring Wi-Fi, high-back seats and handy USB charging points. Each vehicle also includes two wheelchair spaces. 710e (SF74 YMJ), on its first day in service, picks up passengers at Blackford station on 8 September 2024.

At an investment of more than £24 million, Lothian's commitment to introduce cleaner, greener buses into the fleet underpins one aspect of a much wider strategy to achieve net zero emissions by 2035. The business has already taken massive strides in fitting the necessary infrastructure at its main depot in Annandale Street to support the charging of the vehicles, with future plans to 'electrify' the company's other depots as set out in Lothian's 'Driving towards Net Zero' environmental strategy. MCV Volvo BZL 707e (SF74 YMJ) in the grounds of the Royal Infirmary of Edinburgh on 8 September 2024.

Originally planned to commence in 2020 prior to Covid, five Stagecoach East Scotland Alexander Dennis Enviro200Avs became autonomous buses. The long-awaited CAVForth project autonomous route AB1 finally commenced in May 2023 linking Ferrytoll Park & Ride in Fife with Edinburgh Park station via the iconic Forth Road Bridge with most of the route not requiring a driver. Stagecoach East Scotland Alexander Dennis Enviro200AV 62003 (YX69 NUP) reaches the Edinburgh Park terminus on 15 May 2023.

Ember Yutong electric TCe12 SG71 OTA charging up at Wallyford Park & Ride on 15 May 2024 before setting back to Dundee. Ember operate a number of express services with electric coaches including one between Dundee and Edinburgh (E3) with some extended journeys (E3X) to Wallyford on 14 May 2024.

Acknowledgements

My grateful thanks go to my friend and 'all things transport' expert and popular author Gavin Booth for providing a foreword for this book. Gavin, of course, has written some excellent transport books covering his home city of Edinburgh, which I would encourage you to look out for if you haven't already done so, especially his extensive and very comprehensive *A Century of Edinburgh's Transport and Buses* – a 144-page hardback book that was published in 2024. I would highly recommend you get a copy if you haven't already done so. Thanks also to Steven Oliver for providing dates and background information that have helped considerably in preparing this book.

If you would like to see more scenes and vehicles from all of the Lothians and examples of types not featured in this book, some of my other titles from Amberley Publishing might be of interest as Lothian is featured heavily in all: *Lothian Buses: 100 Years and Beyond*, *Buses in All-Over Adverts*, *The Buses of East Scotland*, *Route Branding and Special Liveries on British Buses*, *The Bus and Coach Today*, *The Use of Vinyls on Buses and Coaches*, *On Trial: Bus and Coach Demonstrators* and *Demonstrators and Touring by Bus and Coach*. My own hardback titles – *Seeking the Perfect Location: Trials and Tribulations of a Bus Photographer* and *Scotland's Buses: The Road to Net Zero* – they also contain many rare Edinburgh images from the 1970s to modern day.

I am writing these acknowledgements with a mixture of emotions. My journey with photography over the years has led to me meeting some fantastic people both within the enthusiast circles but also within the bus industry too and who have become great friends. The year 2024 saw the retirement of George Balloch and Alan Rintoul, both splendid chaps who will be sadly missed by their colleagues in Lothian Buses, Airlink and East Coast Buses. And, sadly, another employee and lifelong bus and ambulance enthusiast, David Mitchell, passed away suddenly during the year. This book is dedicated to his memory.

Finally, a big shoutout to all the current providers of bus services. It's not an easy task, I know, and to keep buses and trams running to time with ever increasing challenging roadworks and sometimes limited staffing resources making things extremely difficult. The annual International Edinburgh Festival and Fringe is itself a perfect example of the city becoming particularly busy. Many changes have occurred since the 1990s. What will be to come?

All the photos in this book were taken by myself. Wherever possible I have included the dates when photos were taken as an aid to identifying the constant changes between the 1990s and today.

Just as I was finishing compiling this book, the National Transport Awards for 2024 were announced with Lothian named Bus Operator of the Year and Edinburgh Trams named UK Tram Operator of the Year – proof if you should need it that Edinburgh Public Transport is up there at the top in the country. Also Lothian Buses' City Sightseeing Edinburgh tour was named the best in its worldwide portfolio of tours by City Sightseeing Worldwide and Thomas Gilhooley of Lothian East Coast Buses won the UK Bus Driver of the Year Competition, held in Blackpool on 1 September 2024.